Lifelong Loyal Clients

How Smart Professionals Turn **Relationships** into **Revenues**

Deb Brown

INDIE BOOKS
INTERNATIONAL

No part of this publication may be reproduced or distributed in any form or by any means without the prior permission of the publisher. Requests for permission should be directed to permissions@indiebooksintl.com, or mailed to Permissions, Indie Books International, 2424 Vista Way, Suite 316, Oceanside, CA 92054.

Neither the publisher nor the author is engaged in rendering legal or other professional services through this book. If expert assistance is required, the services of appropriate professionals should be sought. The publisher and the author shall have neither liability nor responsibility to any person or entity with respect to any loss or damage caused directly or indirectly by the information in this publication.

ISBN-10: 1-947480-29-4
ISBN-13: 978-1-947480-29-2
Library of Congress Control Number: 2018952968

Designed by Joni McPherson, www.mcphersongraphics.com

Author photo by Laine Torres Photography, www.lainetorres.com

Contents

To my family.

To those who came before me and paved my path.

To those who walk beside me and share the path.

To those who come after and follow in my footsteps.

You'll always be first.

"By small and simple things are great things brought to pass."

Alma 37:6

PART I

Loyalty Matters

1

Why Two of Three Clients Leave

The customer's perception is your reality.

KATE ZABRISKIE

W hen you lose clients, they probably give you excuses. They don't have time. They don't have money. They are going in a different direction.

Here is the hard truth: They may not be telling you the real reason.

According to the Customer Experience Report by RightNow[1], the number one reason clients leave a business is because they believe the business doesn't care about them. In fact, 68 percent of all clients who leave do it for this reason.

When I talk to small business owners and service professionals, they overwhelmingly beam with pride about their clients. They are proud of the results their clients

---

[1] Kota, Satish. "Why Customers Leave a Company." Infographic. *ReputationXL*, July 11, 2015. http://www.reputationxl.com/charts-infographics/68-of-customers-leave-you-if-you- dont-care-for-them/

achieve. They look forward to working with them. It doesn't sound like a bunch of capitalists who are only in it for the money. These people really care. So why do two out of three clients believe they don't care?

I believe that most businesses *do care* about their clients. But they may forget to let their clients know how much they are appreciated. They are so busy doing what they do in their business, client appreciation and nurturing business relationships falls off their to-do lists. It just doesn't get done.

If 68 percent of clients who leave believe the business doesn't care, but the businesses really *do care*, then we should be able to improve that statistic.

Transaction versus Relationships

For a small business owner, every transaction is exciting. Each transaction means more cash flow and revenues, the ability to pay your bills, and keep doing what you are doing. All the big and little transactions add up to the freedom to run your own business.

While transactions are important to keeping a business afloat, each transaction contains potential. It contains potential for more transactions. It holds the potential for a lifelong loyal client.

Consider a trip to your local grocery store. You go

because you needed certain items—maybe bread, milk, eggs, or produce.

Scenario number one. You find what you need, so you know the store can fulfill your needs. You go through the self-checkout lane and interact with no one. The odds of your returning are pretty good because they have what you need. There are probably several other grocery stores nearby that can also provide what you need. You will probably visit a different one each week depending on which one is on your way home or which is open when you need to purchase something.

Scenario number two. You find what you need, so you know the store can fulfill your needs. You also got great service—someone helped you find something, a clerk made you aware of a coupon you were eligible for, somebody carried your groceries to the car. You are more likely to return because you feel cared for. If they have an extra incentive—like a punch card or five dollars off your next visit—it will give you even more reason to return.

Both visits to the grocery store got the job done. In the first scenario, it was nothing more than a transaction between you and the store. In the second scenario, the store built a relationship with you. Building a relationship takes more effort and manpower. It costs a little more to the store.

It will also make more money for the store in the long run.

In your business, you are probably getting the job done. That is transactional thinking. One transaction can turn into many if you focus on building a relationship with your clients rather than just fulfilling a transaction. The initial investment of time and money is higher when you focus on relationships, but in the long term you save money on marketing costs and grow your bottom line through repeat business.

Show Them That You Care

If two out of three clients who leave believe you don't care about them and you are ready to change that, you need to be strategic and intentional about how you show appreciation to your clients and nurture your relationship with them. If you show your clients you appreciate them, it adds value to your business relationship. It gives them more than just the services they paid for.

In the book *The Five Languages of Appreciation in the Workplace*, Gary Chapman and Paul White share how appreciation is best expressed in business.[2] The basic concept is that as individuals, we each have a preferred way of receiving appreciation. When someone uses that method, we feel appreciated. When someone expresses their appreciation

---

[2] Chapman, Gary D., and Paul E. White. *The 5 Languages of Appreciation in the Workplace: Empowering Organizations by Encouraging People.* Northfield Pub., 2012.

in another way, we may not recognize it. According to their work, there are five different ways to express appreciation.

Physical Touch

Physical touch can be expressed in many ways: a handshake, a high-five, a pat on the back, or a hug. In the context of personal relationships, this is very important to some people. Chapman found that most people don't desire physical touch as a form of recognition in a business setting. They preferred one of the other languages of appreciation. But humans need physical touch, so don't be afraid to use it appropriately in your business relationships.

Receiving Gifts

Some people feel appreciated when they receive a thoughtful gift. It is a great way to show appreciation to your clients. If you are going to send a gift that will make an impression, it needs to be relevant to your client's interests. A meaningful gift shows that you took the time to know your client and understand what that person would want to receive.

Words of Affirmation

The words "thank you" can be powerful. Some people need to hear or see the words along with *why* you appreciate them. We don't say "thanks" or give compliments often enough. Sometimes our clients need to hear it. Send a note in the mail. Call and thank them on the phone. Give a sincere compliment. Thank them for their business.

Quality Time

In our busy world, some people just want to spend a little time with you. When you meet with clients on the phone or in person, give them your undivided attention. Ask about their personal lives, not just business. Do they have plans for the weekend? Are they planning a vacation? How are the kids? Take the time to get to know each client as a person.

Consider taking them out to lunch—not a business lunch, just for fun. Take them to sporting or cultural events. Host a client appreciation event where you can spend time with all your clients in an informal, nonbusiness setting.

Acts of Service

Some people really feel appreciated when others serve them. Acts of service say, "You are important enough to me that I want to help you." In your business relationships, you can do this by going above and beyond in the work clients have hired you to do. Give them free advice or do something that comes easy for you from your area of expertise, but may be a struggle for them. Provide clients with templates, forms, or instructions that will simplify their lives. When you see a need that you can help with, offer to do it for them.

Because you may not know how your clients prefer to be appreciated, incorporate all of these things into the way you do business. Shake their hands, tell them you appreciate them, spend time with them, send a gift, and go above and beyond. When all of these things happen in your business, your clients will feel appreciated by you. When you do that, they trust your ability to deliver and they will remain a loyal client.

So What?

A business with lifelong loyal clients is more stable. Customer churn rates are lower. It can depend on ongoing business and frequent referrals to sustain it and help it grow. The secret to having that for your business may be as simple as taking care of your clients, which means not just completing the tasks required for their projects, but letting them know they are cared for. It's a simple problem to solve.

2

Take Care of Clients and the Money Follows: The WOW System

In a crowded marketplace, fitting in is a failure. In a busy marketplace, not standing out is the same as being invisible.

Seth Godin in *Purple Cow*

Before we dig into the details of The WOW System, which is the method to create lifelong loyal clients, you're probably wondering how I became a relationship marketing expert.

As a mom of five kids, I spent many years staying home with them. I was nurturing relationships with these little people, who were all unique individuals. Eventually, I started a business that would allow me to be my own boss and work with my kids by my side. I began a personal assistant and errand service. I knew people needed extra help with day-to-day tasks like shopping, taking in the dry cleaning, and picking up prescriptions. I could do all of that for them and I could drag the preschoolers along with me.

I also intentionally created a system to make each client feel special, taken care of, and appreciated. I started out by delivering a chocolate chip cookie with every order. People loved it. It was that little extra thing that made them feel special. But then I realized that not everyone enjoys chocolate chip cookies. I had some clients who preferred a salty treat or a healthy snack. I began customizing how I appreciated my clients. I found out up front what their favorite treat and their favorite flower was. Every week, I would deliver their favorite treat, and once a month I would bring their favorite flower.

My clients enjoyed receiving the cookie, but they were *delighted* when I brought their favorite thing. That small custom detail, which cost less than twenty dollars a month per client, made them feel like I truly understood them and their needs.

One day my client Kim, who was also a small business owner, said to me, "You do such a great job making me feel special. I want all of my clients to feel that way, too. Can you help me do that?" I realized there is a real need to help business owners appreciate and care for their clients. About this time, I was also running myself ragged. I was constantly on the run with other people's errands. When we walked into a store, my kids would ask, "Are we shopping for us or for a client?" It was time for a shift.

As I researched further, I realized that most clients feel underappreciated and because of that, they leave the business. I found that business owners want someone to help them show appreciation to their clients in a way that brings them tangible outcomes—retention and referrals. As I learned and studied and grew as a business owner, I discovered that there is potential in every business relationship to increase revenues. If you take care of your clients, but forget about them after a project is done, you lose repeat business and referrals. When you take your strategic partners for granted, you receive fewer referrals from them. If you don't properly nurture your prospects, you'll make fewer sales.

When I learned the statistic that 68 percent of clients leave because they believe the business doesn't care, it made me mad. Most of the business owners I associate with started their business to help others. They aren't greedy capitalists. They really do care about their clients. They just get busy doing what they do, and although they have good intentions, client appreciation falls to the back burner. Independent business owners struggle with balancing what they do and having the time and cash flow to do it.

I thought, "This statistic shouldn't exist. We should be

able to completely wipe it out, one business at a time, by creating a plan to intentionally show our clients that we care." I didn't believe each gift needed to be high-end; it just needed to be high-impact. If you can think about who your clients are and what your business does for them, you can find a way to thank them that will be meaningful without being expensive.

As I pulled this all together, I hoped that what I was teaching would really work. I was so excited when I received my first international client from Australia. Jane was a leadership expert who was looking for ways to nurture relationships with corporate human resources (HR) leaders and executives. We created a plan that reflected her brand in surprising ways. She came away with ideas that delighted her. As she implemented the plan, she found that those little things made a huge impact on the people she was connecting with. That was when I knew it would be a success.

The WOW System

I continue to help businesses increase sales conversions, grow their referrals, and boost client retention and reactivation. Although for each relationship there is a different way of doing that, it all boils down to the three basic steps of The WOW System.

STEP ONE: Welcome. The way you initiate the client relationship makes a big difference. First impressions matter. Doing this well sets the stage for every other interaction you will have. Your prospects' first impression of you is often established before you ever make contact with them. Your first personal interaction is important. The way you conduct your initial sales meeting or strategy session will influence how they feel about working with you. Welcoming clients involves an intentional process of onboarding and reassures them of their investment. Likewise, when clients complete their work with you they are welcomed into their role as graduates or alumni of your program or project. This sets the stage for referrals and repeat business. Strategic referral partners are welcomed through your initial one-to-one meeting, where you get to know each other and look for ways to help each other.

STEP TWO: Ongoing Outreach. Staying top-of-mind with people requires repeated contact with them. Whether you need to stay in front of a prospect for several months or a former client for years, it is important to have a strategic plan for ongoing outreach. With prospects, ongoing outreach is called follow-up. You must be diligent in following up until your prospects have made a decision one way or another. Once prospects become clients, they still need ongoing friendly outreach to help them feel appreciated. Former clients will completely forget about you if you don't have a system set up to keep in touch with them on an ongoing basis. In order to stay top-of-mind with referral partners, you need to reach out to them every single month.

STEP THREE: What's Next? Everything you do should be leading to what's next for them. For prospects, that is a sale. Clients are led to results and the next service option you have to offer them, or graduating to become alumni. You can lead former clients back to work with you again and to share referrals with you. For referral partners, the next step is the reward they receive when they give you a referral. Whatever role these people are in, if you show them what the next step is, it is easier to get them there.

Now I'm helping clients through this process. I help them do the little things that set them apart as a business. When you are intentional about your business relationships, you help your contacts get to know you, like you, and trust you. That leads to more business. Relationships are the foundation of a long-lasting business. Relationships are what produce lifelong loyal clients.

Part II

How to Turn Relationships into Revenues

3

With Prospects

When given the choice, people will always spend their time around people they like. When it's expedient and practical, they'd also rather do business with and buy stuff from people they like.

GARY VAYNERCHUK IN *THE THANK YOU ECONOMY*

L eigh* is a hard worker. She grew up on a farm. She is a financial planner who also happens to be a millennial.

Putting a younger person in charge of your retirement funds can be scary. It is hard to earn some people's trust. They may think that once they put their money and trust in her, they will never hear from her again. As one of many financial planners in the area where she practices, she knew she needed to do something to stand out.

She had called on one particular prospect thirteen times over the course of a year with no results. She knew something

---

* All the examples in this book are based on true stories. Names and some details have been changed to protect their identities.

had to change. She knew she could help him if she could just get through to him.

Leigh heard about my snail-mail content program through a webinar. Each month I sent her ideas that she could use to send to people in the mail. She personalized them and sent them to the people on her list.

But mailing things was costing her both money and time. At one point she said, "Listen, I'm just starting out. I don't have a big marketing budget or a huge team of people to help me. Sending these things in the mail costs money and takes up so much time. I'm just not sure it's worth it. Besides, none of it has anything to do with financial planning. I'm a serious professional and I'm not sure it makes sense to send fun things in the mail."

I assured her that being consistent and persistent with friendly snail mail would pay off in the end. She thought about that prospect who wasn't returning her calls. Since leaving voicemail messages wasn't working, she figured it wouldn't hurt to try sending things in the mail. She sent a card with a silly cartoon on the front, along with a cheesy fake mustache for Humor Month in April. Lo and behold, the man's wife picked up the phone and called her. She said, "Hi, Leigh. I know you've been trying to get hold of my husband. We have a lump sum of money we would like to invest for retirement."

Once Leigh had a chance to sit down with the couple, she was able to roll over $400,000 in retirement funds from the husband and another $400,000 from the wife. In addition, she was able to give them security through long-term care insurance for both of them, even though the husband had a preexisting medical condition that made him uninsurable on his own. Now they have a nice retirement nest egg along with peace of mind in case of a medical hardship in the future.

They loved working with Leigh so much that they referred her to both of their sons, who have since invested with her and referred their friends, as well. The couple also has connected her with some of their friends. Leigh says, "I attribute it all to that mailing about Humor Month. When phone calls weren't working, sending that piece of fun snail mail got their attention. It had nothing to do with financial planning, but it paid off exponentially for me."

The moral of the story is: it doesn't have to be about business to earn you new business.

The Prospect Puzzle

Have you ever met someone for the first time with whom you connected well at a business or social event, and by the end of the event you felt like you had made a good acquaintance? That acquaintance has the potential to become a stronger connection for you. What happens if the next time you have contact with that person is six months or a year later? If you are like me, you probably will have forgotten his or her name by then. Sometimes it feels a little awkward seeing this person again because you are trying to remember who he or she is, and how the two of you first connected.

A prospect's introduction to your business is much the same. There may be a good connection initially, but unless the relationship is nurtured, the prospect will soon forget about you. Sales don't result just from connection, but repeated connection.

How many touches does it take to close the sale? You will hear different answers to this question depending upon your industry and sales cycle. According to MarketingWizdom.com, 80 percent of sales are made after the fifth contact, yet only 12 percent of sales people make more than three contacts.[3] Take a look at your sales funnel and see how often your drip marketing is connecting with your prospects.

Prospects come to your business in a number of ways. They may enter through the internet, by referral, from a networking meeting, or an expo or trade show. These leads are valuable and varied. The one thing they all have in common

[3] Clay, Robert. "Why 8% of salespeople get 80% of the sales". MarketingWizdom.com. June 13, 2017. https://marketingwizdom.com/archives/312

is the need for you to follow up with them. And that is where the puzzle begins. *How* do you follow up? *How many times* should you pursue them and *how often*? What if they don't get back to you? With all the "noise" in our world, how do you know what will be most effective in reaching people?

I hear from some people that they are horrible about responding to voicemail. They say it takes too many steps. You have to call your voicemail, have a pen and paper ready, write down the message, hang up, and then call the number back to respond. I have called people whose voicemail message says if you want a faster response, please send a text.

These days, texts are easier for people to view and respond to, but it is hard to leave a lengthy message. Not to mention, it can be hard typing into a tiny smartphone keyboard. If you have a few points to address, a text will automatically be divided into multiple texts. If you use the voice-to-text option, you have to be sure to proofread before you send. And watch out for autocorrect changes that can substantially (or embarrassingly) change the meaning of your message.

Email can also be effective, but keep in mind people get many emails each day. And then there are those moments when email gets lost in cyberspace or sorted into a spam folder—or even worse, you thought you sent it, but it actually was just saved to a draft folder.

Sending messages via social media requires the use of third-party website or apps in order to communicate with each other.

If you send something in the mail, the open rate is much higher, but the response rate may be lower and it takes longer to hear back from the person.

Which Form of Communication to Use?

We all have our comfort zone and our default when it comes to communication. When you are following up with prospects, your favorite form of communication is less important than theirs. If you want the best response, you need to use your prospect's favorite form of communication. Here are some tips to help you do that:

1. **Use multiple forms of communication**. If you call and don't hear back, try email the next time. If you still don't hear from them, try a different way of reaching out.

2. **Pay attention to how your prospects first contacted you.** If your first contact came through a Facebook message, chances are that is the best way to get in touch with them.

3. **Give time and space between outreaches to allow**

them time to respond. People are busy. It may take a week for them to get back to you.

4. **Don't give up until you get a clear answer.** A clear answer is, "Yes," "No," or "Not right now." If the timing is off, ask them when they would like you to follow up next.

5. **Determine how frequently you should follow up.** A daily phone call may be overdoing it. Waiting six to twelve months may mean they have forgotten you and moved on.

Follow up can take many touches. Your business is more important to you than to anyone else, so it is your job to initiate and continue the follow up. Your persistence will pay off as long as you approach it from a friendly, caring point of view rather than being pushy and annoyed when you don't hear back from someone. Think of it as a gentle tap on the shoulder, reminding the prospect that you're there.

If you include all these outreach methods (email, social media, phone calls, snail mail) in your follow-up plan, you will be sure to connect with your prospects in at least one of those ways.

The other piece to connecting with your prospects is consistency. People are quick to forget about a business they haven't heard from in a while. The more often you connect with people, the more likely it is that they will remember you.

To convert prospects to clients, they have to know you, like you, and trust you. It takes time to build rapport. Prospects rarely invest at the first meeting. The higher the investment in your services, the longer the sales cycle. Clients need time to prepare for the investment as well as time to determine if they feel comfortable with, believe in, and fully trust you.

Buying your book for twenty dollars is not a big deal. People can make that decision on the spot. If they don't like the book, they are only out a small amount. Investing in your $10,000 coaching or consulting program will require a bigger financial commitment, time commitment, and trust commitment. They will want to minimize the risk of that investment by taking time to research and verify that your program is a wise investment.

If you sell to an organization with many employees, it will take even longer to get approval and finalize the sale than if you are selling to an individual. Knowing the typical length of your sales cycle will help you know how to follow up appropriately.

Welcome Them Quickly

When you first receive a lead, speed is of the essence. Whether you met the person through networking or at a trade show, it is important that you make contact quickly, before he or she has had a chance to forget you. You can send an email or make a phone call to invite the prospect to connect with you further. Remember, no one wants to be sold to. Make this connection—whether in person or on the phone—an opportunity to get to know each other, and explore whether you have services that the prospect needs. Have a conversation and then see if it makes sense to take the next logical step with you. This exploratory conversation is a way for you to welcome this person as a prospect, provide a deeper understanding of who you are, and make a good first impression of your services.

After you have had a deeper conversation, you will find out if this prospect is interested in your services. There will either be a clear yes or no, or the response will be some form of "not right now."

If the answer is no, you can delete that person from your prospect list and move on. If the answer is yes, you can move into your onboarding process. The puzzle emerges with the vague answers like, "not at this time," "maybe later," and "I'll have to talk to someone else before I can make the decision."

When you get one of those vague answers, *ask when your prospect would like you to follow up*. Then enter it into your CRM system or calendar and do it.

If that date is months or a year away, it is important to keep in touch with them in the interim. Imagine if you told someone you would be ready for his or her service in a year and then you had no contact for a year—would you remember that person? Over time, without any contact, people will forget about you. They probably don't want to think of you as the salesman breathing down their necks and stalking them every month, either. That's why you need a keep-in-touch system that is friendly, not salesy. You want to be remembered without being annoying.

Ongoing Outreach

You need to follow up with a purpose. If you are calling a prospect every thirty days, you'd better have a good reason. An awkward phone call stating you are "just checking in" when this person clearly said he or she wasn't ready to work with you for many more months feels uncomfortable for both parties. If you have new information, met a mutual acquaintance, or found something interesting to share, you can call to let the prospect know. The same thing goes for email. If you have a reason to send an email, by all means, do it. If not, then skip it.

Phone Calls

We have become so accustomed to connecting virtually that sometimes we are afraid to pick up the phone. The phone has become the realm of telemarketers, and no one wants to talk to them. So we assume no one wants to talk to us, either. I was following a post on Facebook where people were asking about making phone calls. The opinions ranged from "more personable" to "annoying" and "predatory."

Warm Calls versus Cold Calls

Cold calling has been proven to be quite ineffective. Picking up the phone and dialing everyone in the phone book, or even everyone in an organization won't bring good results. Narrow down your calls to people who have shown an interest in some way. Did they click on a link in your email? Did they indicate an interest on Facebook, but didn't follow through? Were they interested when you spoke at a networking event? When you call people who already have a connection with you, you are less likely to come across as annoying or predatory.

Avoid Being Pushy

No one wants to be that annoying salesperson. You can make phone calls without coming across as pushy. The first thing I always ask is, "Is this a good time?" Nothing is worse than receiving a phone call when you are on your way out the door or waiting for an important phone call and then getting stuck listening to a long-winded pitch. Asking if it is a good time gives them the option to bow out and schedule a better time for you to call. It shows them that you are considerate and respect their time.

Engage in a Conversation

I hate phone calls; I love conversations. Telemarketers have a bad rap because the call is a one-sided pitch. When they ask questions, they are generally insincere. The latest thing is the friendly sounding prerecorded telemarketing robot that pauses after asking questions to make it sound like it is a live person. When you make phone calls, take the time to ask about them. They won't care much about you unless they know you care about them.

Snail Mail

A great way to keep in touch over an extended period of time is through snail mail. Sending fun and friendly things through the mail on a regular basis will brighten your prospects' day while keeping you top of mind. Don't send coupons, business cards or requests for referrals. Send things that will be of interest to them. Whether it is an article that will help them understand your industry or a friendly card, make sure your mail is the most interesting thing in their mailbox. It won't make them feel like they need to reply to you. They won't feel that you are trying to sell to them. They will simply feel that you remembered them and that will cause them to remember you. If you have done this on a regular basis, they will welcome your phone call when they said they would be ready to move forward.

Getting Your Foot in the Door

Some prospects are hard to reach. They don't return your emails and phone calls. Maybe they screen contact through a gatekeeper. If you know this could be a valuable client, it is worth it to do something outrageous to grab their attention. You may have heard of examples like sending just one shoe with the statement, "Trying to get my foot in the door." I have also heard of a cactus with the message, "I don't mean to be a thorn in your side." Another person sends a large nail with a note saying, "Let's nail down a time to get together."

Even if you aren't sending a big outrageous novelty item in the mail, you can get your foot in the door by consistently sending friendly mail. When they open your mail month after month and see that you are consistent and not going anywhere, it increases trust. Eventually, they will want to get in touch with you because you have been in touch with them. This kind of mail is most effective when it isn't boring technical jargon from your industry. Often your clients and prospects don't really care to know all the details as long as *you* know them. That's what they will hire you for. They want to receive something they can relate to.

Seal the Deal

Similarly, when you have a prospect who is close to pulling the trigger, but just not quite ready to commit, you can use snail mail. Send something that will grab this person's attention, like a high-impact gift with a personal note to help this prospect make his or her final decision.

This is a "seal the deal" gift. It is going above and beyond to bring attention to yourself and your business by putting your attention to the prospect. But it has to be done in a way that is not self-promoting. It needs to be all about the prospect. Sometimes this can be just the thing you need to help seal the deal for a really big contract you are trying to close.

When you do something like this, make the gift highly personalized. Take the time to find out about the individual you're sending it to. If you've been in a sales conversation with this person, you know a few things about him or her already and should be able to cater to those likes and interests. Give something that will set you apart and totally wow this future client. When you do this, your prospect won't think about working with anyone else, even if there are multiple proposals to consider.

This technique can also be used if you're trying to persuade someone to do something to help your business. If it's going to be a huge advantage for your business, you want to make sure that it's a huge win for that person as well. You may need to go that extra mile to persuade and convince. That's a great time to send a "seal the deal" gift. It should be something out of the ordinary and highly personalized that speaks to him or her as a person. When you do that, it sets you apart from the others who delivered a proposal. It shows that you care. It shows that you are taking the time to go above and beyond. It shows that you're someone that person would like to work with.

The methods of follow-up are the pieces of your puzzle. The next step is to put them together. Create a step-by-step plan that you can follow and repeat over and over again. Until you do, your puzzle is just a bunch of scattered pieces.

What's Next for Prospects?

All of these follow-up methods should be leading to what's next for your prospects: the programs and services that will best meet their needs. If you follow up for an extended period of time, their needs may change. By staying in the conversation and asking questions, you will be able to provide the best solutions for them.

Invite!

How would you feel if your best friend had a party but forgot to invite you? You would be hurt and disappointed. You would feel like you missed out. Approach your phone calls as an invitation to participate with you. Not everyone will be able to make the party, but you want them to know they are invited. When your prospects hear your voice, feel your enthusiasm, and know that you want to include them, they won't be offended. They will be more likely to sign up because they have received a personal invitation.

4

With Clients

"Studies show that it costs six times more to get a new customer than it does to keep an existing customer. That's why our focus has always been on better servicing our existing customers."

JACK MITCHELL IN *HUG YOUR CUSTOMERS*

James works in life insurance. He realized that the churn rate is high in insurance. Most people never hear from their insurance agent again after they sign up for a policy. He didn't want to be that kind of agent. He wanted his clients to know that he has their backs. After he heard me speak, he approached me and asked for help. He said, "I know I need to take care of my clients, but I don't know what to do and I'm not good at that sort of thing."

I worked with James to create a strategy for reaching out to his clients on a regular basis. We decided to send greeting cards about every other month. In the cards, we shared some of the company values and some personal things about him.

After he got married, he sent a card with a wedding picture and told his clients a little about his wedding and honeymoon.

After we had sent a few mailings, James hesitated. He said, "I know I should do this, but I just hate putting out more money. It costs so much every time we send it out." I explained to him that he was making an investment in future business.

Sure enough, every time he sent one of these friendly mailings, he heard from some of his clients. Some of them needed to upgrade their policies or add another product. Other clients referred him to friends and family members. In the end, his investment paid off.

The moral of the story is: Taking care of your current clients is an investment in future business.

Loyalty Secrets

According to Harvard Business School, a mere 5 percent increase in retention will increase profits anywhere from 25 percent to 95 percent.[4] Clearly client retention has a bigger impact on the bottom line than acquiring new clients. Bain & Company (a leader in global business consulting) reports that repeat customers spend more with a company— up to 67 percent more in months thirty-one to thirty-six than months

[4] Reichheld, Frederick F., and Phil Schefter. "The Economics of E-Loyalty." *HBS Working Knowledge*. July 10, 2000. https://hbswk.hbs.edu/archive/the-economics-of-e-loyalty.

zero to six.[5] Taking care of existing clients is a faster path to cash than pursuing new clients. Long-term clients spend more and refer more. Knowing this, smart business owners focus on retaining customers.

According to a study done by customer experience consulting firm Walker, by the year 2020 customer experience will be more important than price or product to customers.[6] The experience the customer has determines their loyalty and retention. Client retention makes a huge impact on your bottom line, but it also makes your job more fun when you have ongoing relationships with your favorite clients.

Initially, most businesses focus on what they do and how they do it. It is easy to become wrapped up in internal processes and the way things have always been done. If you want to know how to retain customers, you need to step outside your own processes and consider what it is like from the customer's perspective.

Welcome

Often, businesses focus on prospects. They give attention, nurturing, and lots of touches to bring prospects through the

---

[5] Baveja, Sarabjit Singh, Sharad Rastogi, Chris Zook Zook, Randall S. Hancock, and Julian Chu. "The Value of Online Customer Loyalty and How You Can Capture It." Bain & Company.

[6] "Bring Your CXinto the Future." Walker - Customer Experience Consulting. Accessed April 19, 2018. https://www.walkerinfo.com/.

sales process. Sometimes, when they come to the end of the sales process and make the sale, business owners breathe a sigh of relief and then stop paying attention.

Onboarding is a key point where you can change the way you do business and make a big impact on your clients. Clients, at that time, may be feeling a little bit apprehensive about the investment they just made. They may be feeling excited about starting to work with your business, but if you stop the communication, the excitement wanes and they may be a little unsure about what comes next.

Intake

Having a formal intake process can not only assure you have vital information like contact details and billing information, but also be a great way to start getting to know your clients. As you interact with your customers, continue to pay attention to details about them and about their lives. It's those personal details that help you get to know them better and deepen your relationship with them. What are their hobbies, their families? Do they have kids, grandkids, or a significant other? Are there things going on in their extended families? Do they have parents they are caring for? All of these little details are very important to them, and when you pay attention to those details, you find out what matters most to your clients.

Touching your clients' hearts and really WOWing (The WOW System) them is the best way I know to build loyalty in your business. There are five things you should know about your clients so that you can WOW them in a personal way.

- *All* **Contact Info.** We live in a virtual world and sometimes never meet face to face with clients. Other times, clients come to our place of business. It's easy to think that the only information you need is a phone number and email address. Take the time to also get their mailing address. Having all this information opens up multiple ways to reach them that they probably aren't expecting. If you don't collect all their contact information, it makes it difficult to reach out to them. Getting a snail-mail address allows you to put things in the mail to stay in touch with them.

- **Their Birthday.** Unless you are in health care, you don't need to ask for the year they were born. Take the time to get the month and day of your clients' birthdays. It is the one day of the year that belongs only to them. Just having this information gives you the ability to reach out to them when they aren't expecting you to.

- **Who Do They Care About Deeply?** Most people

have someone who is important to them, be it a significant other, children, parents, siblings, pets, or a close group of friends. They probably sacrifice for them and spend most of their free time with them. Knowing who is most important to each of your clients gives you a way to connect with them on a different level. It can direct your conversations and gives you the opportunity to show an interest in the people in their lives.

- **What Are They Passionate About?** Are there hobbies, activities, causes or organizations they spend their time with? Knowing what is important to them and what brings them joy helps you know them better as individuals. One client may have a hobby like knitting, gardening, or fixing up old cars. Another may be passionate about a sports team. Some people fill their spare time with volunteer work to support causes that are important to them.

- **How Do They Indulge Themselves?** For some people, a piece of chocolate or a cup of coffee is the thing that makes them happy. Others enjoy a massage, going to the theater, or reading a book. Still others love an adventure like rock climbing, zip-lining, or mountain biking. Knowing what your clients would do to treat themselves allows you to customize how you reward them.

How Do You Find This Information?

While knowing these details can help you build a relationship with your clients, you don't want finding it out to feel like an inquisition. You can learn some things a little at a time, but making it a part of your onboarding process is the easiest and most unobtrusive way to collect the information.

Whenever clients begin work with a new business, they expect to supply information so the business can set up the account and begin working with them. Adding a few more details to the process will feel very natural to your client. You can give them the form to fill out, you can send them to an online form or survey, or you can ask the questions over the phone. Make it as easy as possible for your clients to give you the information.

What to Do Once You Have It

Now that you have more information about your clients, use it to your advantage. Ask them about the people in their lives during your conversations. Make note if they have aging parents they are caring for or children involved in activities. Ask about their best friend's wedding. Then continue to show interest and concern about those things. Talk to them about their passions in life. Find out about their latest project, what book they are reading, or their volunteer work.

When their birthdays come around, send a card or a gift. And when you want to send a gift—for a birthday or to celebrate their accomplishments—send them something they would love to indulge themselves with or something that relates to their passions. It becomes so much more meaningful when you personalize it, and your clients will be wowed.

There are all sorts of ways to use this information. If you just pay attention to the details, you can incorporate those details into your gift-giving and your interactions. Take time to ask your clients about those things in their lives. That will deepen their relationship with you and cause them to appreciate you as a businessperson. When you have a stronger relationship with clients, they stay with you longer, and if they stay with you longer, you make more money.

Welcome! Welcome! Welcome!

The beginning of the client relationship is a great place to put a little extra effort into customer service. Now that you have gathered some information about them, it is time for you to welcome them. It might be as simple as a welcome email that explains the process that you work through and the steps your clients can expect. Let your new clients know what you need from them to get started. Tell them what they should expect to see from you. Those kinds of communications give clarity to the relationship and make them more excited to work with you. If you stop nurturing the minute you make the sale, then you're losing their interest before you even start working with them. Make sure you do a little something to keep the relationship alive.

You've heard how important first impressions are. Although your new clients already know you, you are now making a first impression of what it is like to work with you and your business. They've just "joined a club." You might not have a secret handshake, but now is the time to make them feel like they made a good decision and that they are part of an elite group.

From the buyer's point of view, there is something that often happens after making an investment. (The bigger the investment, the more likely it is to happen.) Buyer's remorse sets in. The buyer questions whether or not he or she made the right decision and wonders if he or she will get what was paid for. There may be a sinking feeling in the buyer's gut as he or she questions what was just committed to.

When new clients sign a contract with you for six or twelve months, they are making a big commitment. When they're just starting out, they don't know what the results are going to be. There is no guarantee that they will see a return on investment. But if, soon after they sign on the dotted line and commit to you, they experience your welcome process, it can help reassure them.

You can turn your clients' fears of the commitments they just made into surprise and excitement by sending welcome gifts or packets. When they receive something that tells them you can't wait to start working with them, they will anticipate even better things from the work you will do together.

Having a great onboarding process means a smooth transition for new clients. It has the potential to make them feel welcome and reassured that they made the right decision. If you are a practitioner who works with patients, your welcome may be in the form of a new patient information folder. Clients in a low-cost program may just receive a note in the mail. For high-investment, private coaching or consulting clients, you may do something bigger like a welcome package in the mail. A great welcome process can also encourage your new client to refer you to others.

Imagine your brand-new clients receiving a package in the mail from you. They open it first because it is the most interesting piece of mail in their mailbox. As they open it and look through it, they find informational pieces and testimonials that reassure them they made a good choice.

But there are also unexpected surprises and freebies that are useful and catch them off guard. There are also some helpful items to share with a friend so that your client becomes the hero—sharing valuable resources.

This welcome package has a two-fold purpose. First, it creates a great first impression for new clients. It makes them feel welcome and gives them value, which also helps combat buyer's remorse. Second, it is an easy way to spread your brand.

The welcome package is valuable because it:

- Reassures new clients that they made a good choice
- Surprises them and makes your business stand out
- Gives instant value, sometimes before you even begin working together
- Provides them with a permanent reminder of you
- Gives them a reason to share with their friends and associates (referral with no pressure)
- Shows them you value their business
- Strengthens your business relationship right from the start

Here are some things to include:

- Welcome letter
- Testimonial sheet

- Important information, procedures, and policies for working with you
- A useful promotional item that pertains to them and to the work you do
- Something of value to pass along—tip sheet, valuable coupon, or discount

The welcome letter, testimonial sheet, and policies and procedures may feel like standard operating procedures, but sending them in the mail is probably different than what most companies are doing. When you choose a promotional item that will be permanent and useful in their environment, it will continually remind them of you. The promotional product will keep your business top-of-mind, and others may see it and ask about it. The tip sheets and coupons make it easy for clients to share with their friends so you will receive referrals.

Receiving a package will make new clients feel special and important to you. The surprise and delight that comes from receiving something unexpected will increase their excitement and anticipation to work with you. Now, instead of that sinking feeling of worry when they think of your business, they will feel joy because you cared enough to go out of your way and send them something. If they were considering trying to back out of their commitment before, they are less likely to do so now.

Ongoing Outreach

When you are in the thick of a client relationship and you've been working together for months or years, clients can start to feel taken for granted. Clients stay with the businesses that care about them, so there must be an ongoing nurture of the relationship. Here are some significant times you can concentrate on.

1. Your client's birthday
2. Recognition
3. A yearly holiday
4. Ongoing "little touches" that make the experience of working with you more special
5. The halfway point
6. Client appreciation

Birthdays

As part of your intake process, you have already collected your clients' birthdays. The next step is to enter that information in your calendar so you don't forget it. You may want to add a reminder a few weeks ahead of the date to buy a card or gift and get it sent in time for the special day.

An important caution: To make a big impact, this needs to be all about them. If you send a card with your business card in it, *it's no longer just about them*. It becomes about you promoting your business. If you send them a card with a special sale for them for their birthday, it's about them buying from you, not about you giving to them. You have to keep this a gift if you want it to be appreciated.

Celebrating your clients' birthdays is a great way to stand out. If this type of client gifting is done the right way, it will increase client retention and word of mouth referrals. The key is to focus it on the client's birthday and not make it about your business.

Recognition

Not long ago, I was talking with a colleague who had joined a large group program led by a well-known guru. Due to the size of the group, she didn't have direct access to the group leader, but the group leader was a big part of the reason she joined. As she participated in the online forum, she shared and celebrated an accomplishment. Soon she received a card and a gift in the mail congratulating her— from the group leader. Her reaction was, "She noticed me."

Being noticed by the group leader meant a lot to her. It made her feel directly connected in a group where she could have been lost in the crowd. That feeling of connection caused her to rave about the program she was in. (It was great free advertising for the group leader which leads to referrals.) The recognition also made her feel a degree of attachment to the leader and the group that made her want to renew her membership for the next renewal cycle. (Client retention equates to higher profits and less work filling the program.)

No matter what business you are in and no matter the size of your client list, clients look to you as an expert and celebrity. They wouldn't work with you if they didn't admire and believe in you. Imagine the impact it would have on your business if each of your clients felt noticed by you. When you take the time to notice their accomplishments and be interested in who they are as people, clients feel more connected to you. We like doing business with people we have a connection with. We feel loyalty to businesses that care about us.

If you want to increase connection with your clients, start noticing things! There are so many things you could notice. Keeping track of birthdays is just the beginning; pay attention to life events like marriages, new babies, kids going off to college. You can even notice the sad events, like the loss of a loved one. Watch for milestones and accomplishments. Did your client win an award or celebrate twenty-five years with the company? Taking the time to write a quick note or send an appropriate gift is a huge gesture that will touch your client's heart.

Yearly Holiday

A great way to brand your business and set it apart is to introduce your own holiday. If you think about the holidays when you're expected to give gifts, you probably immediately think of December. When December rolls around, you're scrambling, thinking, "What do I give to my clients?" You probably feel pressure to recognize your clients.

The problem with sending gifts in December is they don't stand out. A million people are sending gifts in December, and they're not only from businesses, they're also from friends and family. Your gift basket or your gift card just get mixed in with many other gifts. It's hard for people to remember who gave them what at the end of the holiday season.

Another problem with December is that not everyone celebrates the same holiday as you do and some people may be offended. Wishing your Jewish clients a Merry Christmas may not go over well, and some people may actually celebrate neither.

If your purpose for giving gifts to clients is to appreciate them and make a memorable impression on them, give your gifts at a time that will stand out from everybody else. That's why introducing your own holiday can be a strategic move for your business. Find a holiday that aligns with your business, with your message, and with your values. Make that your business's custom holiday and celebrate it every year. You can also celebrate your company's anniversary each year instead, just as long as it's not near the winter holidays.

There are holidays for doctors, lawyers, financial planners, and insurance agents. Everyone Deserves a Massage Day and No Housework Day exist. There are many holidays every day of the year. If you can't find the right one for you, you can create and submit your own holiday.

Search online to find one that fits your business. Once you've picked your holiday, customize a fun gift that will capture the attention of your clients and prospects. A meaningful gift at an unexpected time stands out and makes a much bigger impact than sending a holiday card in December. It will make your business more memorable. And who do people do business with? The business they remember.

Little Touches

Sometimes the biggest surprise comes from something small given at an unexpected time, for no reason at all. Random notes of appreciation, cards at an unusual time, or a small gift to brighten your client's day can help them feel cared for by you. It may feel random to your clients, but you can plan for it in your business. You may choose to do something quarterly as a part of your ongoing outreach. Your relationship with your clients will be filled with pleasant surprises and they will know you appreciate them.

Halfway Point

If you've ever been involved in a group program, consulting contract, or a project, you'll probably recognize the cycle that these go through. In the beginning, people are filled with excitement about the opportunity and the journey they're beginning on, new people they're connecting with, a new leader, and new possibilities. As the experience progresses, energy starts to fizzle. People lose enthusiasm somewhere in the middle. By the end of that experience, there's a bittersweet ending. Often it's gratitude and joy for the experiences and sadness that it is over.

Whether you run groups or just work on a project basis or on retainer for a specific amount of time, you need to combat that fizzle in the middle. You need to give the participants a reason to participate and stay engaged. If you can keep the enthusiasm high, then participants are more likely to reenroll, or sign another contract. Continuity is huge for your income.

The key to increasing engagement is to make sure that participants feel connected to you and to the other members of the group. Some of this may be facilitated by social media groups and emails, but don't forget about other ways of engaging people. Think about picking up the phone and reaching out to participants, especially if you see that they aren't actively participating.

Consider putting together a sequence of snail mailings that go out to all your ongoing clients. It might be something small, like a card every other month with a message from you. It could be something a little bit bigger from time to time, a low-cost gift, or even a higher-cost gift, depending on how much your clients are investing. If you plan ahead, you won't be scrambling to reengage participants in the middle of their contract. You will be keeping them excited and engaged throughout your work together.

When they receive something personal from you in the mail, it helps them know that you care about them and that they are important to you. When they feel that you are interested in them, they become more engaged and stick with the program. The group as a whole feels more bonded, and everyone has a better experience. When it comes time to start the next group, there will be an increase in returning participants.

Client Appreciation

You want your clients to feel like they got their money's worth and more. There are some ways to do that without spending a lot of extra money. One way is to give appreciation. If you show your clients you appreciate them, it adds value to your business relationship.

Thank-You Notes

Thank you notes are a great way to share words of appreciation with your clients. Some people wonder how soon you need to send a thank-you note. Often, you may feel that if you don't send it out right away, it's too late and then you've lost the chance. It doesn't matter when you send it out—it matters more that you send it out.

An interesting thing happens when there has been a delay between the work done and the thank-you note sent. The clients had time for you to fall off their radar and get busy with their lives. When you send thank-you notes in the mail, it brings you back to the top of their minds. Sometimes this actually leads to new business or referrals. When you remember them, it causes them to remember you.

You shouldn't send a thank-you note with the intent to get more business, though. Your clients will feel your ulterior motives and be turned away. Sending a thank you with sincerity and authenticity will be well received from your clients. It won't always result in new business, but it will set you apart and put you top of mind with former clients.

Client Appreciation Gifts

Client appreciation gifts are a great opportunity to reinforce your brand and strengthen your connection with clients. Showing your gratitude to clients through an appropriate gift elevates your business in their eyes, but there is a right way and a wrong way to do it.

If a gift is done right, it will create a buzz. Clients will be so delighted that they'll take a picture of it. They'll post it on social media and say, "Look what I got. This made me feel special." It gives them a reason to talk about your business in a good way, which can lead to referrals. If a gift is done right, it will cause them to want to stay with you and do more business with you. They will feel that you care about them, and that should be the real purpose of a gift.

Even if referrals don't come right away from social media, the goodwill of sending out a kind gift and showing your clients you care can still result in referrals. Later, when they're talking to friends who need whatever it is you do, the first person they're going to think of is you, because you showed them kindness.

The Wrong Way

Some businesses order large quantities of branded promotional items and then hand them out as if they are gifts. Business owners love their brand and their business. When they see their logo printed on something, it feels magical to them. There is a sense of pride—like showing off new baby photos. Close friends and family may be impressed, but to the average person, it's just another marketing piece. Hand them out at trade shows, but please don't call them gifts.

When your logo is on a gift, it is considered a marketing piece, not a gift. The only time you should give it as a gift is if you work in an industry that has strict compliance policies about how much you can spend on gifts for a client. If you are going to add your logo, I have a couple suggestions:

1. **Make sure the item is still related to your business.** If every business gives out a pen or a coffee mug with its logo on it, it no longer stands out to the receiver.

2. **When possible, personalize it to your client.** Add the client's name or something that means a lot to this person.

3. **Make the logo subtle.** If you are giving it as a gift, you want the gift to be the center of attention, not your business.

It's ironic that, when you remove your branding from the gift, it still builds your brand image. People will still associate the kindness and goodwill with your brand, and that is good for business.

Other businesses take a product that they sell and give it away for free. This makes a great bonus, but if it is your own product, it shouldn't be given as a gift. A gift needs to be all about the recipient, not about the giver.

Another approach involves coming up with a nice, generic gift card that will appeal to everyone. Sending out Starbucks gift cards may seem like the easy way to show a little love, but it won't make a big impact. It is a step in the right direction, but if you are using your business budget, you want more than a nice gesture; you want something that will be memorable.

A Better Way

You can connect your gift to your brand *without* branding it with your logo. Think of words or images that you use frequently in your branding and incorporate those into your gift. Maybe you are known for a certain word, phrase, or quote that you use with your clients. Sharing that on a gift will tie the gift to your brand in a way that will be meaningful to your clients. You might use a certain flower or animal as a metaphor for the work you do. When a client receives a gift that incorporates that symbol, it will be a meaningful connection to you and your business.

A gift should reflect your brand personality. An edgy, in-your-face company won't reach their clients by giving them a hug and sending flowers. A nurturing business that touches people on a personal level won't be well served by sending their clients an irreverent gag gift.

Your clients have something in common. They come to you because of the problem you solve. When you give a gift that is related to what you do, it will remind your clients of you and reinforce your brand.

If you have a product that you *love* and it relates to the work you do, that can make a great gift. Think of Oprah's favorite things, but for your tribe.

Take the time to give meaningful gifts that relate to your brand. When you do that, it will be more memorable and make a bigger impact on the recipient. When you make a big impact on the recipient, it will make a big impact on your business in return. You will see an increase in client retention and referrals.

When Gifts Are Illegal

Before you give any gifts, be aware of any laws or regulations around gifting in your industry. Some industries are tightly bound to not give gifts. If you are in education, health care, or similar industries, you may not be able to give gifts. Other industries have limits in place that restrict spending for gifts. Even though you may be limited as to what you can do, it's still important to find some way to show your clients you appreciate them. This will make you stand out from the crowd.

So, how can you show appreciation if it's illegal or you have a very small budget to spend? One way to get around the issue is to add your logo to whatever item you're giving to the client. As soon as you add your logo to a gift, it becomes marketing material and not an actual gift in the eyes of the government. This is great; it helps you comply with regulations while still doing some nice things for clients.

If you are bound by laws, find an appropriate way to show appreciation to your clients. Don't cross any boundaries, but let them know you care.

Client Appreciation Events

Hosting an annual event for your clients can be a great way to show them you appreciate them. Events give you an opportunity to spend quality time with your clients. It can also be a great way to encourage referrals as you invite clients to bring a friend.

The ideas for customer appreciation events are endless. Just make sure to plan something that your audience will look forward to attending and will be thrilled to invite a friend to. That way you have the opportunity to be introduced to potential clients and your existing clients can easily refer their friends to you in a nonthreatening way.

Customer Service

Every once in a while, something will go wrong in your business. You might make a mistake, a vendor you work with might goof up, but the bottom line is it causes a problem for your clients. It is important to apologize and take care of the problem. When something goes wrong, you break the trust that your client has in you and your ability to deliver your service.

The good news is recovering from mistakes can actually earn lifetime loyalty from the client. It's like an unexpected test. When something goes wrong, the client's first instinct is to be upset at the injustice. That's understandable. When you handle things correctly, so the client is happy in the end, they will be more loyal to you than they were before.

When problems arise in your business, they provide an opportunity for you to increase loyalty. We know that unhappy clients tell more people than happy clients. According to Lee Resources[7], 70 percent of customers who complain will do business with you again if you resolve the problem in their favor.

---

[7] "75 Customer Service Facts, Quotes & Statistics." Infographic. *Help Scout*, May 28, 2012. https://www.slideshare.net/helpscout/75-customer-service-facts-quotes-statistics/25-FACT_91_of_unhappy_customers.

According to research from Accenture Strategy, 67 percent of customers would stay with a business if their issue was resolved on the first call.[8] Recovering from mistakes gives you a chance to gain more loyalty than you had before. The fear of making mistakes is unfounded. The opportunity is real. Recovering from a goof-up in your business requires you to do a few simple things.

Take the time to communicate with those clients who are unhappy, and very often you can turn them from unhappy clients to lifelong loyal clients. They are more likely to stay with you if they know that you're going to take the time to understand them and communicate with them, even if things don't always go right. If clients feel they are treated fairly, they may become your biggest advocates, despite the problems they experienced. When clients are unhappy, the business relationship is damaged. A damaged relationship can cause clients to go to your competitors.

If you ignore a problem and don't acknowledge it, clients will find someone else whom they feel they can trust. They will seek out a business that isn't going to fall down on the job. If you go through these steps to acknowledge what you've done wrong and assure them that it won't happen again, clients

---

[8] Wollan, Robert et al."Exceed Expectations with Extraordinary Experiences." Accenture. com. December 20, 2017. https://www.accenture.com/t20171220T024439Z__w__/us-en/_ acnmedia/PDF-68/Accenture-Global-Anthem-POV.pdf#zoom=50

will be very forgiving and willing to work with you again. It's a matter of integrity to step up to the plate when you've done something wrong and apologize.

Apologizing with a Gift

Sometimes, you make one mistake and you can apologize and move on. Once in a while, however, you may feel the need to do a little more. It may be a mistake at the beginning of the relationship and you want to reassure your new client. Or perhaps you made a really *big* mistake. It may be that you have dropped the ball more than once. If you need to apologize in a bigger way, it might be a good time to send an "I'm sorry" gift.

It isn't necessary to send a gift every time you make a mistake. Often a simple apology in person or over the phone is enough to fix what went wrong. An email or personal note in the mail can add to your sincerity. Don't overdo it. Once the other party has forgiven you, it is time to move on and let it go. You shouldn't bring it back up and continually apologize for something in the past.

When you know that you've really broken the trust of the person you're working with and they're not very happy, you need to do something to make up for it. That's the time when it is appropriate to send a gift to smooth things over and let them know that you are sincerely apologizing for whatever has happened.

An "I'm sorry" gift doesn't necessarily have to cost a lot; it depends on how big the mistake was. The act of going the extra mile and sending something out to say you are sincerely sorry can do a lot to repair the trust you have broken. You are showing your customer that you acknowledge whatever you've done to mess up his or her day or to take up his or her time. You understand the value of time and you're willing to pay for it.

When you take the time and effort to apologize with a gift, it goes a long way in repairing a situation. You are able to reestablish trust and that person is willing to try again with you. Hopefully you've learned your lesson and you won't make the same mistake again.

What's Next for Clients?

While you are doing a good job of taking care of your clients, you should also be looking ahead to their next steps. If you work with clients on an ongoing basis, this will be their contract renewals. For businesses that work on a project or program basis, it may be leading them to the next program or project that you can help them with. It might also be your clients "graduating" and becoming alumni. Sometimes clients aren't aware of all the things you do that you can help them with. As projects or contracts come to a close, be sure to share with them other opportunities to work with you. If you have built loyalty, they are likely to want to continue working with you.

5

With Past Clients

Are your customers resigning or re-signing?
JEFFREY GITOMER

Amelia owns a web design firm. She works very closely with clients as they build their websites. When the websites are completed, she needs to give her time and attention to the next client. Because of this, she was losing touch with her past clients. She also felt that her projects were incomplete because she never formally thanked her clients. Knowing that your best new clients often come from former clients, she didn't like the fact that she was losing touch.

A while back, she assessed the situation. She knew something had to change.

She approached me with the desire to do something not only going forward, but also retroactively for past clients. We put together a plan to send a low-cost gift to past clients. We created custom notebooks for each of her clients with their brand on it.

Because she had so many past clients that she wanted to thank, it seemed a little daunting. How could she afford to do this for all these past clients? They weren't paying her anymore, so she didn't have the budget for it. We decided to send a few each month until she caught up with all her past clients. The results blew her away!

"Doing the notebooks has actually really affected my bottom line," she said. "People are reminded about me and I become top of mind. Last month I had someone call because I sent them the gift and they hired me to do more work. It happened again this month. Each time it has more than paid for my investment. I'm getting more business because I'm sending the notebooks. And that's not even the reason I'm doing it.

"It has always been my goal to let people know how much I appreciate them, yet with all the tasks that keep my attention all day, it can be difficult to put in the thought and care that I really want. Deb understands this, and she comes to the rescue. The gifts that I give my clients are intentional, personal and my clients feel the appreciation that is meant for them—and it absolutely continues to grow my bottom line."

The moral of the story is: if you don't remember them, they won't remember you.

Reactivation Riddle

Have you ever finished a good book and didn't want it to end? You become involved with the characters' lives and don't want the story to be over. You hope that there will be a sequel so you can stay connected with what happens next.

You may feel that way about clients as well. When you work closely with someone, that person can become a friend. You have connected with him or her personally and professionally. And now the contract, the project, the program is over.

Past clients are a great source of repeat business as well as referrals. According to Sweet Tooth, repeat customers' sales conversion is nine times higher than a new prospect.[9] You can position yourself to create a "sequel" with the clients you love. Not only will it mean income for your business, but more importantly, a chance to work with, connect with, and help your favorite clients.

Whether it is the end of a project or program, your contract is up, or a client decides to move in a different direction, there are times when you must part ways with a client. As a business owner, this can bring mixed feelings. You may be delighted for the time you had to serve them

---

[9] McEachern, Alex. "Repeat Customers Are Profitable and We Can Prove It!" Smile.io. Accessed April 20, 2018. https://www.sweettoothrewards.com/blog/repeat-customers-profitable-stats-to-prove/.

and are ready to let them move on. There may also be a part of you that is concerned about the loss of income. Losing a client can feel disappointing.

Ending on a positive note allows clients to return when their situation changes. If you do a great job and give great customer service, chances are good that your clients will come back. They may leave because they have been wooed by the promise of lower prices, but they will return when they realize the quality they are missing. When you take it personally and get defensive, clients won't want to come back to work with you. If they end their work with you on a sour note, they will also try to prevent others from having that experience. When you end with class, on the other hand, it leaves the door open for your past clients to return and refer you to others.

Welcome

Saying goodbye and ending client relationships is actually welcoming them into their new roles as former clients or alumni of your business. Consider how a college keeps in touch with its alumni after graduation. They want to celebrate their accomplishments and encourage their continued support of the college. You can do the same thing with your former clients. They can be your best advocates— referring and promoting you to others. And somewhere down the road, they may be ready to come back for a reunion or a graduate degree (a.k.a., another event, project, or program).

We often hear about how important it is to make a good first impression, but endings can be just as important in your business. An ending is the last chance you have to make an impression, so make it a good one. The impression you leave at the end of a program, project, or contract will be the last thing your clients remember about you. Ending well involves closure. Wrap up assignments and make sure you have completed those things that were promised to your clients in a timely manner. Do it well and set the stage for them to come back and work with you again.

The "welcome" process for your alumni should include three main things:

1. Completing projects and programs

2. Getting feedback

3. Thanking them for their business

Completing Projects and Programs

Graduating clients should feel supported during the transition. Don't try to use your power of persuasion to change their mind. Change isn't easy for anyone, and the clients have put thought into this before they came to you with the decision. Let them know you support them and want what's best for them. Make sure you complete any projects or assignments that you have agreed to do. Just because clients are leaving doesn't give you permission to put them on the back burner. This should be the time you put out your best work so they realize just how much you do for them.

Getting Feedback

When clients stop working with you, it may be for a number of reasons. As a business owner, you may think you know, but unless you take the time to ask, you don't have all the information. When clients end their service, they most likely give you an excuse for moving on. Often, those excuses are just a way to be polite. To get to the root of the problem, you need to ask questions through a client exit survey.

The first question you should ask is why they are leaving. It might not be the reason or excuse they gave you. Knowing this information alone can help you make changes in your business to increase customer retention.

Find out what they liked and what they didn't like about working with you. This information can open your eyes to things that may be very simple to change, but will create a better customer experience. Ask them how satisfied they are and how likely they are to recommend you to others.

Keep the survey short and sweet. People don't want to spend a lot of time, but they usually do want to give you their opinion. Some of the questions should be multiple choice for quicker answers, but leave some questions open ended to allow clients to tell you things you might not be aware of. This is also a great opportunity to ask for testimonials and referrals.

Net Promoter Score

You can use the data from your exit survey to figure out your Net Promoter Score (NPS). NPS is a score of how loyal your customers are. The question you need to ask is, "On a scale of one to ten, how likely are you to recommend our company to a friend or colleague?" From that question, you can calculate the NPS score for your company. Here is how it works. Scores fit into one of three categories:

1. **Promoters.** These clients chose a nine or ten on that question. These are the people who are highly likely to tell others about you. They are the most loyal customers.

2. **Passives.** They chose a seven or eight in answer to the question. Passives are satisfied with your business, but not delighted enough to open their mouths and tell others.

3. **Detractors.** They chose anywhere from zero to six. They range from dissatisfied to slightly satisfied. Because of this, if they tell others, they are probably sharing a negative story about you.

The more promoters you have in your business, the more your business will grow organically from word-of-mouth referrals. To figure out your NPS, you find the percentage of each category—promoters, passives, and detractors. Then you subtract the percent of detractors from the percent of promoters.

The number can range from a negative number to 100, if every client was a promoter. The aim should be in the 50 to 80 range. You can locate standards for different industries online or with a little assistance from your local librarian. For example, the average NPS for internet service providers is a 2, but the average for hotels is 29. If you look up your industry, you can find a benchmark to aim for. More important, work to improve your NPS each year within your company.

Tracking and knowing your NPS gives you great insight into how your customers view your company. It helps you track loyalty and likelihood of referrals.

How to Administer a Client Exit Survey

The easiest way to administer a survey is to put it online. There are services available to build and host surveys like Survey Monkey or Google Forms, or you can house it on your own website.

If your clientele is not tech-savvy, consider a paper form that you ask them to fill out on the last day of service, or mail to them later. Make it easy for them by providing a self-addressed, stamped envelope so they can return it to you.

You can also interview your clients at your last meeting. While talking with them may generate good conversation and insights, they may also hold back and not want to be completely honest to your face. You can hire someone outside of your company to call and ask the client exit survey questions on your behalf in order to get more accurate information.

Having a client exit survey helps you gather information so you can do more of what your clients like and improve the things that aren't going well. If you find that the client is leaving due to problems with your business, you have the opportunity to apologize and fix the problem. Understand, of course, that doing so may be enough to keep that particular client with you. If there was no fault on the part of your business and the client is leaving for reasons outside of your control, respect their decision.

Thanking for Business

If you end by thanking clients for their business, their last impression of you will be that you appreciated them. Appreciation can range from a handwritten note to a more substantial gift.

You can send a simple card that says, "We appreciate your business. We enjoyed working with you and we hope we can serve you again in the future."

If the client is leaving because it is the end of a contract, project, or program, it is the perfect time to send a parting gift. This gift should be something permanent that will add value to your client. Consider what the client would like to receive rather than what you would like to give.

By giving something permanent and lasting, you will stay in clients' lives as they look at or interact with the gift. Even if you aren't interacting regularly anymore, they will think of you when they see the gift you gave.

Ongoing Outreach

When you stop working with someone, they don't have a reason to think about you anymore. The house is sold. The furnace is repaired. The graduation party is over. Their need for you has passed, and so you aren't on their mind. Even if they had a great experience working with you, as more time passes they may even forget your name.

If you want them to remember who you are, you need to keep in touch with them. This is easy to do with ongoing clients. If you work with them every week or every month, they will naturally remember you because they see the appointment on their calendar or receive the emails from you.

It takes more effort to stay in touch with former clients. The more time that elapses from your work with your clients, the more likely they are to forget about you. Reaching out on a regular basis to see how they are doing will keep you top of mind and make them feel comfortable returning when the timing is right for them.

There are a variety of ways to keep in touch with your past clients. They may receive a regular newsletter or e-newsletter from you, but you can't guarantee they are opening your emails. It is important to remember a more personal touch as well. Call them on the phone. Interact with them in person. Send a personal email or message through social media. Don't forget to send things in the mail. While an email might not be opened and a phone call may result in voicemail, physical mail from someone you know is almost always opened. Mailing things to past clients on a regular basis is a gentle way of reminding them that you are still there and available for business. If you don't remember them consistently, don't expect them to remember you when they are ready to hire again.

Knowing how long before they will need your services again will help you determine how long and how often to stay in touch with them. A furnace and air conditioning company may service clients a couple times a year, while a real estate agent's clients probably won't need their agent again for ten years. You need to communicate frequently enough that they will remember you and you can earn their repeat business. You want them to think of you first when they need your service again, but you don't want to be an annoying stalker who is constantly bothering them.

Snail Mail

Cards are a great way to keep in touch with prospects, clients, and partners. If you want to be remembered, annual holiday cards for business aren't enough. I have heard that if you haven't communicated with someone for a month, then they have already forgotten about you. It probably depends on how deep the relationship is, but there is a lot of truth to that. If I don't talk to my mom or sister for a month, don't worry, I'll still remember them. But, if you are an acquaintance, a colleague, or a businessperson whom I have only met casually, I may forget you. You see, my brain needs reinforcements. Go ahead and send your holiday cards for your business. I can't wait to get one in my mailbox! But if you want to be remembered, also send things throughout the year.

You can also send informative newsletters in the mail if they contain information that the recipients will be interested in reading. If you already have a blog, simply repurpose those articles in printed form. Writing a letter that updates clients on what you are doing is another way to keep in touch with them.

Take the time to remember birthdays. You can send a simple card or one that includes a small gift or incentive to visit you again. One client I worked with started sending birthday cards to everyone on her list with an invitation to come into the office for a free gift. She gave a small item of value while they were there and invited them to schedule an appointment.

What's Next for Past Clients?

To keep your clients longer, make sure you have something to offer them. If they finish one program or project, is there another program that will serve them next? They are probably enjoying working with you. If you have a next step for them to take, they may gladly move into your next program.

A common practice among coaches, consultants, and healers is to create packages to offer to clients, rather than billing by the hour. It is a great way to offer your services. Clients know what to expect—how many sessions, what you will work on, and what the cost will be. You can offer several different packages (small, medium, and large) to accommodate different needs and budgets. The negative side to offering packages is that they come to an end. Whether it is six weeks or six months, you eventually reach the end of your agreement. Ending your work means you don't retain clients.

If you have done your job well, your clients may not want to completely let go of you, but they may not have the need or the budget to invest in another package. Creating an ongoing monthly maintenance plan is a great way to keep your favorite clients coming back to you, create an ongoing income stream, and give clients exactly what they need—you in a smaller package.

You can't retain clients if you have nothing to offer them at the end of their package or program. Here are some ideas:

1. **Maintenance Plan.** If you work intensely for a period of time on a weekly or every-other-week basis, create a package in which you meet once a month for a shorter time. You can help with new problems that have come up and continue the growth they started. This can be used for therapists and personal trainers.

2. **Alumni Group.** For graduates of a program you offer, you can invite them to an alumni group. Everyone has received the same training and is working on

a particular skill set. Through the group, you can address needs, brainstorm, and members can hold each other accountable. This method works great for trainers and coaches.

3. **Support and Implementation.** Is there a piece of the work you do that you could lend ongoing support? Think of the little things that will sit on their to-do list, but not get done. This could be used by marketing and social media consultants, web designers, or home services.

Creating an ongoing package for your clients increases your ability to retain clients because you have something to offer them. You make more money, they get better results, and loyalty increases with long-term relationships.

If you don't have a way to create a continuity program in your business, you may have an annual update or review you can offer them. You can invite former clients back. This might be through a personal phone call letting them know you enjoyed working with them in the past and you have a current opening. It could also be a special direct mail campaign encouraging past clients to come back. (Think of the coupons you get in the mail when you haven't been in to get your hair cut in a while.)

Annual Events

If your clients aren't ready to work with you again, or if you are in an industry where you know they won't need your services for years, invite them to an annual event. This can be a client appreciation event for all your former clients. It gives them a way to connect with you at least once a year even if they don't need your services yet.

Reunited and it Feels So Good

In our family, when we know we will see each other for a holiday or vacation, the anticipation builds. We start getting excited about being together, and we make plans. When we are finally reunited there is such joy.

Reuniting with former clients can bring the same excitement and joy. You already understand each other and are familiar with each other's backgrounds. Working together again is something to look forward to.

A former client who already has an established relationship with you will be an easier "yes" than the new prospect who is just now trying to decide about you. Bringing former clients back can be a great source of income for your business.

6

With Referral Partners

Even though your referral sources may be willing and able to refer you, you still need to help motivate and stimulate them.

JOHN JANTSCH IN *THE REFERRAL ENGINE*

uanne is an estate attorney, a likable solo professional who has grown her practice over many years. She has found that the best way to grow her practice is through referrals, and the best referrals come from financial planners. Through networking, she is always seeking to meet financial planners. Sometimes she hits it off with them and finds a new referral source. Other times, nothing ever comes of the connection. She realizes that you can't force people to give you referrals. It has to be something that they want to do, because they know it will benefit them as well as their clients.

After years of connecting with financial planners, Luanne was frustrated. Certainly, she knew should be getting more referrals with all the connections she had. That's when she was referred to me by someone in her networking group.

We spoke on the phone about her desire for more referrals. She had the right connections but wasn't receiving the volume of referrals that she could handle. We came up with a plan to send fun and friendly things by snail mail to twenty-five of her strategic partners on a monthly basis.

The first month or two, nothing happened. Luanne began to question the strategy. Some of the things we sent in the mail had nothing to do with estate planning or financial planning. How could a greeting card help her get more referrals? I assured her that it takes time and repeated connections to nurture business relationships.

We continued sending mail to her twenty-five strategic partners. Lo and behold, after the fifth mailing things started happening. People who had never sent her referrals started referring people to her. One strategic partner also invited her to be a presenter and get in front of a larger audience.

After a difficult Minnesota winter, she sent a card that said, "Welcome Spring!" to all her referral partners. Shortly after that, she received an email from one of her partners' office assistant telling her how much he appreciated her and the mail she sent to him.

Luanne said to me, "This mail thing really works. It's just human nature for people to forget about you." The moral of the story is: Building business relationships takes time. It's not a one-time event.

Referral Magic

Think of the last time you received a referral. How did it feel? I asked that question on a webinar, and the response was, "Magic." Referrals often come out of the blue. You aren't expecting a referral on that day or at that moment. Referrals feel like magic because:

- They catch you by surprise

- They come with a glowing recommendation from the referrer

- A referral sale is a quicker and easier sale than from any other source

Having predictable sales is important to your business. Sprinkling in some referral magic can be the icing on the cake.

Magic is often associated with a "trick." The reason it's considered magic or a trick is that you're unsure how it happened. The trick happens in a way that defies what you can see. It doesn't make logical sense to the observer, and you can't tell how the magician did it. In reality, the magician has practiced, prepared, and created a background to support the trick.

You can be the magician of your referrals. It may look random and defy logic to the outside observer, but behind the scenes, you can prepare and support what you want to happen—more referrals. It takes time, practice, and preparation, but it can become a logical, repeatable part of your business. You don't have to trick anyone into giving you referrals. You just have to prepare and create a way for the magic to happen.

Are You Referable?

You can put all kinds of systems and incentives in place, but if your business isn't referable, then you won't receive referrals.

When people give you a referral, they are trusting you with someone who is important to them. Their credibility is on the line, and they are vouching for you. They don't want to tell their friends or colleagues to work with you and then have them have a bad experience. That would be embarrassing for them.

Here are some issues that will make people think twice before referring you:

- Overcharging
- Under-delivering
- Too many mistakes

- Lack of communication
- Leaving things unfinished
- Poor customer service

Avoiding these things isn't asking too much. It is just the basic traits of doing good business. If you want to grow your business through referrals, you have to first make sure your business is worthy of those referrals. If it isn't, fix the problems. When you deliver great results along with great customer service, your business will be referable.

Strategic Referral Partners

The Power of a Twenty-Five List. How many people do you know? You may have hundreds of Facebook friends and thousands of Twitter followers, but how many people do you really *know*? I'm talking about the people who, if you saw their names or their faces, you could tell me something about them. Estimates tell us that each person knows between 100 and 250 people. In fact, there is something called Dunbar's number: the number of people you can maintain a relationship with. Dunbar's magic number is 150.[10]

You can't connect deeply with every one of those people, so narrow it down. Just focus on creating a deeper connection

[10] Dunbar, R. I. M. "Coevolution of Neocortical Size, Group Size and Language in Humans | Behavioral and Brain Sciences." *Cambridge Core.* February 01, 2010. https://www.cambridge.org/core/journals/behavioral-and-brain-sciences/article/coevolution-of-neocortical-size-group-size-and-language-in-humans/4290FF4D7362511136B9A15A96E74FEF

with twenty-five of them. If every one of those twenty-five knows between 100 and 250 people, that gives you access to between 2,500 and 6,250 people. If we stick with Dunbar's number of 150, your twenty-five will connect you to 3,750 people. Among those people, what are the chances that some are your ideal clients? Depending on who is on your twenty-five list, the number could be great.

To get access to that database of 3,750, all you need to do is build trust and stay top of mind with your twenty-five list. If your twenty-five list is connected to your ideal clients, then begin focusing on building relationships with those twenty-five people.

You may feel clueless regarding whom you should seek as referral partners, and that's perfectly normal. Sometimes you are just too close to your own business to recognize the opportunities. You may even feel that there is no ideal referral partner for your business because it is unique.

Some businesses are more unique than others, and sometimes it is a challenge to nail down the best referral partner. With a little brainstorming, it is possible to find referral partners for anyone in any business.

Knowing your ideal referral partner starts with knowing your ideal clients. Once you have identified them, you can seek out people who have regular contact with your prospects. If they have access to the same people you want access to, there is a potential partnership. Finding the right referral partners will allow you to receive easy referrals over and over again instead of picking up one or two at each networking group you attend.

How to Find a Good Referral Partner

Even if you find and completely hit it off with someone, he or she may not send you referrals. One of the reasons may be that the person does not have contact with your ideal clients. A good referral partner will regularly run across prospects that could use your service. The best referral partners usually fit into one of three categories:

1. Clients

2. Cheerleaders/connectors

3. Colleagues

Clients can be good referral sources for you. The clients who are most likely to refer new business to you are the ones who got the best results from working with you. These are probably your top 20 percent and the ones who are your raving fans. If they are your ideal clients, they probably rub shoulders with more of your ideal clients. They can easily share your name when one of their friends or colleagues needs what you offer.

Not all clients, however, are good referral sources. If you work in an industry where clients like you to be their best-kept secret, they are less likely to share your name with others. This is often a phenomenon found in industries that are very personal in nature. Whether you deal with debt, emotional problems, or beauty, your clients might not want others to know they are seeing you.

Cheerleaders and connectors are those people who may never use your services, but they believe in you, cheer you on, *and* connect you with others. Often these are the people you meet networking who are natural connectors. When they understand and believe in what you do, they are happy to connect you to people who need your services. These people probably also have a large list of connections, so it is easy for them to connect two people in their network.

Colleagues who see your ideal client on a regular basis are a great source of referrals. The best scenario is when they see your ideal clients *before* they need you, as with Luanne, the estate attorney who found that the best referral source for her are financial planners. Clients get their financial planning done and then the logical next step is to look at their estate planning. Because of this, she is always connecting with financial planners.

Real estate agents regularly see people who want to sell

their homes and may need house cleaning, home repair, or staging services. They also see clients who are buying a new home and need a mortgage broker and closing company.

Sometimes colleagues all work together at the same time toward the same goal and can share referrals among each other. They may work in the same industry, like wedding professionals. The caterer, wedding planner, photographer, and DJ can all work together to share clients because their clients need many of their services at the same time.

A web designer and a graphic designer can work hand in hand to help a business create its brand and online presence. They could also partner with a copywriter and social media manager to help a business with its website copy and marketing.

Keep in mind that just because you send referrals to someone, that doesn't necessarily mean he or she will be able to reciprocate. A financial planner may send lots of referrals to an estate attorney, but an estate attorney rarely has clients who don't have a financial planner. A dentist regularly refers clients to an orthodontist, endodontist, or oral surgeon, but those professionals probably don't see people who need a dentist.

Think about your industry and actively seek out referral partners who have direct contact with your ideal client. They may see clients before they need you, or they may be able to work side by side with you to help the same client in different ways. As you get to know people who have the ability to send you referrals, you will see your referrals increase.

Welcome

The welcome with referral partners starts with a one-to-one meeting. A one-to-one meeting is a get-to-know-you session. As a business owner, you want to promote your business. If you don't, you will go out of business. Since you are also passionate about what you do, sometimes your enthusiasm can overpower others. They may feel that you are only interested in pushing your business. That impression will lead them to not want to do business with you themselves, as well as prevent them from referring you to someone they care about.

How to Have a Powerful One-to-One Meeting. Think about a one-to-one meeting from the other person's perspective. What does he or she want?

Chances are this person wants the same thing you do: referrals and sales. This person wants to attract interest in his or her business:

- **Ask lots of questions.** This keeps the focus on him or her.

- **Find out about this person first, personally and professionally.** Approach each one-to-one meeting as an opportunity to get to know the individual.

- **Ask how you can help him or her.** Look for opportunities to share and help this person move forward in business.

- **Provide connections to other people who will help this person's business.** Do you know of a resource that would benefit him or her (not your own products or services)? Follow up after the meeting with any resources or connections you promised.

- **Put yourself last.** If you have done all of these things, this person will naturally want to turn the tables and find out about you.

Ask if this person has contact with people who struggle with the problem that you solve. You can describe your ideal client and then see if he or she knows anyone who could benefit from your services. You don't have to formally ask this person to be your referral partner. You can simply point out how what you do might benefit his or her clients and ask if there is a way the two of you could collaborate. There are many ways you could collaborate to get your name in front of this person's clients:

- Include a flyer or your contact information in his or her welcome packet or end-of-project resources page.

- Have a joint event for both of your clients—either in person or virtually.

- Offer to give something of value to all of this person's clients—a book, recorded webinar, tip sheet, presentation, or free consultation.

- Be a sponsor for an event that he or she is putting on.

Many times, your referral partners won't even have to know that they are on your list of referral partners. You just have to connect, feel synergy between the two of you, and then continue to build the relationship.

Ongoing Outreach

If you want to be top of mind with your referral sources, you need to communicate with them on a regular basis. You need to plan a way to keep in touch with them monthly in a friendly way so they are continually reminded of you. You can meet them in person, make a phone call, send an email, or use snail mail. There are advantages and disadvantages to each way of keeping in touch with your referral partners.

Contact Method	Advantages	Disadvantages
In Person	You can make a better connection They hear your voice and see you	It takes more time to meet in person (travel time) It costs money (meeting fees, lunch or drink costs)
Phone	They hear your voice It's free If they answer, you can have a relationship-building conversation	You will mostly be sent to voicemail People don't always call you back Some people don't listen to their messages
Email/Instant Message	You can send it at any time day or night, regardless of time zone differences It's free	People's inboxes are overflowing An email will be deleted and forgotten Some emails aren't even opened Some emails end up in spam or lost in cyberspace
Snail Mail	People have to physically interact with a piece of mail It has a higher open rate than email A physical item stays around longer than an email It stands out because other people aren't doing it	It costs money—paper, envelopes, stamps, etc. It takes more time/labor to assemble everything It takes longer to get to the recipient

Why You Should Use Mail

There are many options for keeping in touch, but by now it is probably obvious: my favorite is snail mail. Whether you send a letter, a card, a small gift, or a newsletter, it is more likely that you will get noticed.

Handwritten messages sent through the mail have become uncommon. We're way too impatient to wait a few days just for someone to receive our message. Our mailboxes have become overrun with advertisements and credit card offers. There is rarely something interesting to open in the mailbox. That creates a great opportunity for small businesses to use direct mail.

When you get the mail, you know what a pleasant surprise it is to receive a card, a note, or a letter. Think of the delight your business contacts will feel toward you when you send them something in the mail. Mail to your referral partners should be used to build relationships. Sending out a blast of coupons to people you have never met will put you in the category of all the other advertisers in the mailbox: annoying. It will most likely go right in the trash. But if you use mail to nurture and build relationships, it will stand out among all the other junk in the recipient's mail box.

When you use snail mail to keep in touch with your targeted list of twenty-five referral partners, it is very affordable. You can easily send something for about $1 per person, and you can spend more from time to time to make a bigger impact. How many referrals would you need to recoup a $25 monthly cost? For most business owners, one referral would create a huge return on investment.

There are several things that will make mail stand out:

- Handwriting on the envelope

- The size and shape of a card

- A colored envelope

- A return address from someone the recipient knows

- Something three-dimensional (as small as a little something that fits in the envelope to a full package with a gift inside)

You don't have to do all of these things, but any one of them will make the recipient notice your mail first and open it first.

What to send in the mail. The first thing to establish is the purpose of your mail. The next problem to solve is deciding what to send in the mail. When sending to referral partners, you aren't trying to make a sale, so don't send a coupon or advertisement. The purpose of mail to referral partners is to build your relationship with them and be remembered by them so that they will send you referrals. Think about who your referral partners are and what they would like to receive. Are they interested in valuable information about your industry? Then sending newsletters and articles is a great way to stay in touch and establish your authority. Would information from your industry bore your referral partners out of their minds? Then send something fun instead, like a card or an update letter. Give them something quirky and unusual that will catch their attention, make them think about you and talk about you.

Developing a relationship with referral partners requires repeated contact with them. Because you are nurturing a relationship, you want that contact to feel authentic, not automated.

Automating and having a plan ensures tasks get done in your business, but how do you make sure you contact your referral partners consistently while still coming across as authentic? Here are ways to create an authentic keep-in-touch system:

- **Create a twelve-month mailing plan.** Once a year, plan a full year of mailings. Having a plan in place makes it easier to act on your intentions or outsource the details. Although you will be sending the same thing to all of your referral partners each month, you can add a couple of handwritten sentences to each recipient if you want it to feel more personal. Having an overall plan will make it easier to implement.

- **Set a reminder.** Use your electronic calendar to your advantage by creating a monthly appointment to do it. Block the time each month, and don't schedule over it.

- **Use an automated system.** Signing up for a keep-in-touch system like Send Out Cards (sendoutcards.com/timecreators) is one way to automate. It will allow you to create a campaign that will automatically send a card to the people you choose. You can choose to send monthly, quarterly, or on a specific date, and the system will mail a physical card of your choosing. A physical card with your message in your handwriting will feel more authentic without your having to hand-write every card.

- **Hire help.** Even if you have a plan, you may not find the time to follow through. If you know this task will fall through the cracks, use a virtual assistant or a service like Touch Your Client's Heart (touchyourclientsheart.com). They can implement your keep-in-touch system for you.

However you do it, creating a keep-in-touch system will ensure that your good intentions are acted on. When you make these little things a priority, your referral relationships will grow—and so will the number of referrals you receive. Take the time to authentically automate your efforts so your referral partners hear from you consistently.

What's Next for Referral Partners?

Lessons from Pavlov's Dog. Think for a minute back to when you were a teenager and you were in science class. You learned about Pavlov's dog. If you remember, Pavlov taught his dog how to salivate. He did that by ringing a bell and setting out food over and over again.

This repeated action taught the dog that every time the dog heard the bell, there was going to be food, so pretty soon he could ring the bell and the dog would salivate even when there was no food.

What's next for your referral partners involves rewarding them when they give you a referral.

You need to condition and train your referral partners so that they will give you referrals over and over again. You do this by rewarding the behavior, just like Pavlov did. The dog was rewarded with food. You're going to reward your referral partners by thanking them every time they give you a referral. When that reward system happens over and over, they will learn that you appreciate referrals and that they will be rewarded for it. Determine how you can acknowledge your referral partners. Let them know that you appreciate it and you'll receive more referrals.

Laws, Rules, Regulations. The first thing to keep in mind is whether your industry is bound by laws that would limit how you thank someone for a referral. There may be a "no kickback" rule. This is to prevent shady practices of buying customers. Make sure you know the laws and follow them. If you are restricted, you can still thank someone for a referral by sending a handwritten thank-you note. This lets your referral partner know you appreciate the effort without breaking any rules.

Frequent Referrals. If you are in a business that receives frequent referrals—multiple per day or week from an individual source—it is impractical to send a formal thank you for every single referral. An example would be a mortgage company sending referrals to an insurance agent. The volume can be very high. In this situation, you should acknowledge each referral—most likely by email—so the referrers know you are following up. Then you can thank them in a bigger way, but less frequently. You could buy lunch for their office or hold a quarterly event for all your best referral partners.

Private Work. If you are in a business where you work one-to-one with people at a higher investment rate, referrals will probably be less frequent. Each referral, however, will have a greater impact on your income. If this is your situation, you should thank someone for a referral with a gift that is consumable and repeatable. This means they can be used up by the recipient and they will be happy to receive it again. This could include:

- Gift cards
- Food or drinks
- Flowers
- High-end bath and body products
- Note cards/paper products

The nice thing about choosing something consumable is that you don't have to decide what to send every time. Your gift is repeatable, and that makes it easy for you. It also gives your referral partners something to look forward to.

Like anything in life, you get more of what you pay attention to and appreciate. It only makes sense that saying thank you for referrals is a great way to encourage more. Depending on your industry, you can do different things.

Affiliate Programs. In the online marketing world, affiliate fees are a common practice. You give your promoters a special link that tracks the people they send to you and all sales that come from them. You then pay a commission for each sale that comes from them. If you sell a product or program online, this is a great way to get more exposure. Affiliate partners promote what you have to offer because they believe in you, your product, or service. They get a check as a way to thank them for the new business they brought you.

Referral Fees. In some industries a referral fee, finder's fee or "kickback" is common. Receiving the referral saved you time, marketing dollars, and effort in getting a new client, so giving the referrer money is one way to say thank you for referrals.

Discounts and Credits. If you receive referrals from your own clients, they may appreciate a discount, credit, or upgrade toward your service. You know they appreciate what you have to offer. They must be loyal, raving fans or they wouldn't take the time to tell others. If you offer a service, it won't cost you anything to give this kind of thank you for referrals, but the value to your current clients will be great.

Appreciating referrals is an important piece of any referral program. Give people an incentive to refer and recommend you. If they don't feel their referral was valued, they will often give their referrals to someone else.

You can feel the magic of consistent referrals in your business when you consistently do these few steps. These things will keep your name top of mind with your referral partners. They will feel appreciated and be willing to send you referrals again and again.

Just like any magic trick, once you know how it's done, it isn't so mysterious.

Part III

Sustaining Lifelong Loyal Clients

7

Creating a Loyalty Culture is a Process, Not an Event

Take half your advertising budgets and spend it on existing customers.

JEFFREY GITOMER IN *CUSTOMER SATISFACTION IS WORTHLESS—CUSTOMER LOYALTY IS PRICELESS*

The foundation of everything you do has to reflect the personality of your business. The first step to touching your clients' hearts in a meaningful way that makes an impact is to know your brand. What is the personality of your business? Why do clients come to you and why do they stay? What is it that you give to them? How do you want to make them feel?

As a business owner, you are creating an experience for your clients. The moment you pick up the phone and call them, you are creating an impression. Each impression contributes to their overall experience working with you.

Just like a successful event, if things go seamlessly for your clients, they won't even realize how much work was involved. Making sure things happen seamlessly takes up-front effort on your part. By putting a little thought and planning into what your clients experience, you can create an atmosphere where they want to stay and return again and again.

Taking the time to be kind and ask your clients about themselves personally shows that you care about them as people, not just clients or transactions. As you get to know them, be aware of what is going on in their lives, whether it is stressful challenges or exciting accomplishments. Either way, when you recognize those things and show an interest, it creates a bond and increases loyalty.

Having a business filled with lifelong loyal clients requires a lifelong commitment to take care of them. A single event has the power to surprise and delight someone. A culture that is committed to nurturing relationships will turn prospects into clients, clients into lifelong loyal clients, and strategic partners into cheerleaders and supporters.

This isn't the 100-meter dash. This is a marathon. You have to be committed to making this a part of your ongoing operations. When there are deadlines looming, projects that need to be finished, and fires that have to be put out, this has to be a priority. Set aside time for these activities and assign people to be responsible for them. It can't be the list of "nice to do" things that gets pushed to the back burner. That's what most businesses do, and that is why their clients *believe* they don't care about them.

What to Do and When to Do It

Here are some ways to systematize these activities to make them easier. First, create daily, weekly, monthly, quarterly, and yearly tasks. Some possibilities for these are:

- **Daily.** Write thank-you notes to new clients and prospects you met with for the first time. Make follow up phone calls.

- **Weekly.** Send birthday cards. Follow up with prospects.

- **Monthly.** Send snail mail or pop by with a gift to strategic referral partners.

- **Quarterly.** Send snail mail to clients, past clients, and long-term prospects.

- **Yearly.** Send an annual gift to top clients. Send a yearly greeting card to all contacts. Host an annual client appreciation event.

Keep things as simple as possible. If you are sending a quarterly mail piece to your past clients, you can also include your centers of influence rather than having an extra task that month. Then enter these tasks in your calendar as appointments. As they become part of your routine, it will be easier to stay on top of them.

Setting a Budget

Next, you need to set a budget. If you're not sure where to find the money, take a look at your marketing budget. This is marketing to your closest contacts and will give you a bigger return on investment than marketing to masses of unknown, untargeted people. It makes sense to use part of your marketing budget for relationship marketing. You can also consider how much a client is worth to you. Take a portion of your profit from each client and reinvest it in him or her. You have to be committed to the investment. There will always be something in your business that you need funds for. It is easy to allow other things to take priority and say, "I'll do it next month." When you put these things first, they pay for themselves. You will stretch to send a gift, and you will get new business from it. When you're not sure about sending a mailing to all your past clients, but you do it anyway, you will suddenly get new referrals. When cash flow is tight in your business, find a less expensive option, but do something.

Creating Content

Once you have the tasks created and your budget set, you must create the content. What specifically will you send for your snail mail? How will you recognize birthdays? What will you choose for appreciation gifts? What will you do for your yearly event?

If you are a service provider, much of what draws clients to your business is *you*. Make everything you do an authentic representation of you. Put in little pieces of your personality. Share things about your hobbies, your likes, and your interests.

Some of the things that get the best response have little to do with business. These pieces are meant to build relationships. That means you need to allow your connections to get to know the real you. When you let your personality and brand shine through, you create higher impact without a high investment.

I have sent bookmarks with a list of my favorite books because I love to read. A client who loves to bake sent out recipes for National Baking Day. Another client who wanted to put some silly fun into her business sent crazy straws and whimsical paper hats. A business in the pet industry sends dog treats to her client's dogs to wish them a Happy Valentine's Day each year. Yet another client who has a passion for biking and beer sent out bicycle-shaped bottle openers.

Outsource and Automate

Now that you have a plan of how to nurture your business relationships, you can outsource and automate the details. There are online tools that automate sending cards and newsletters. You can find services that will take care of creating gift baskets, purchasing gifts, shipping packages, and mailing things for you. Just because it is a personal touch, that doesn't mean you have to personally take care of every detail. You can delegate the responsibilities of actually doing it. If you are going to run a business, you can't take care of all these details. If you have an administrative assistant or virtual assistant, they can take care of much of this for you.

Since you've made it to this point, your mind is probably swirling with thoughts and ideas. Thoughts and ideas aren't enough. You need to change what you have been doing, and you certainly can't do it all at once. I suggest focusing on your clients first, because if you don't take care of them, nothing else matters. Add a welcome process or a client appreciation gift. I've offered you a lot of ideas for things you could do. What will you do first to create lifelong loyal clients?

8

And in Closing

People can copy your product, your pricing, your actions, your recipe or program or formula. But they can never replicate who you are.

SALLY HOGSHEAD IN *HOW THE WORLD SEES YOU*

Why do people buy? Why do they leave a business? Why do they stay? Why do they refer? The answer to all these questions is based more on emotion and how a person feels about a business than straight logic. People do business with those they know, like, and trust. Once they have made a decision to work with a business, they stay with the business for results and because of the relationship they develop. If clients are drawn to you because of your personality and *who* you are, then logically this is a big part of *why* they stay. Clients desire a level of intimacy. When they feel connected to you, they feel more loyal. When you show that you are invested in them—that you care about them, take a personal interest in them, and appreciate them—then they are willing to invest more in you.

I can buy phone service, trash service, or internet services from anyone. Because there is no personal relationship with the provider, I base my decisions on cost and results. However, if I am choosing a doctor, a financial planner, a real estate agent, an insurance agent, or another service where I will have personal interaction with the provider I rely heavily on how I feel about the person. Even if I choose a service provider based on my gut feeling that I know, like, and trust the provider, my feelings can change as I work with them. I lose trust through mistakes, customer service issues, and just a general feeling of not being cared for.

If you are a service provider, it's important for you to recognize that these are the issues that plague your industry. Business revolves around relationships. If you don't build a relationship with a prospect, they won't trust you enough to hire you. Once a prospect becomes a client, you need to do things to continue nurturing the relationship, or they will feel you don't care about them. Even when clients complete their work with you, it's important to stay in touch with them. Past clients will often hire you again and refer others to you. Even strategic partners who never hire you need relationship-building.

How does a service professional go about building relationships? If you are a solo professional, you are busy serving clients and growing as a professional, as well as running marketing, sales, finance, operations, etc. There is a lot on your plate. Building relationships is a piece of your marketing—relationship marketing. Make a commitment to add small and simple things that create a sense of surprise and delight for the people you interact with.

You can surprise your clients by timing a gift or card when they are not expecting anything. Sending something when it is *not* a major holiday increases the element of surprise. This might mean you celebrate a lesser holiday (you know—anything that doesn't happen in December!). You might send something for their birthday because they don't expect *you* to remember their birthday. You might send something "just because."

Another way to increase the element of surprise is to give something unexpected. You may be gifting at a time that the recipient expects to receive a gift, but you can give them something they never expected to receive. When a gift is a surprise, it stands out from other gifts received at the same time. It is more memorable. It packs a bigger punch. You can do this by paying attention to the details about your clients. If you know significant things (likes, dislikes, interesting facts from their past), you can use those to choose a gift they would never expect but will totally love.

Go out of your way to serve your clients by doing a little extra for them or introducing them to someone who can help them. These unexpected acts of service can surprise and delight them.

The opposite of the feeling of surprise and delight is when a gift is given out of obligation. It may be the timing (businesses often gift in December out of obligation). It may be a lackluster gift (Oh, look! Everyone got the same gift card!). You can feel the sense of obligation come through in a gift. I know it is the thought that counts, but when a gift is offered out of obligation and there is no sense of surprise, it has a much smaller impact on the recipient.

If you create a systematic way to build business relationships, you will find you focus less on marketing and sales because you keep the clients you have and you receive regular referrals. Not only does this make cash flow easier and more predictable, but it also makes your work more enjoyable. When you have long-term relationships in your business, you enjoy coming to work each day because the people you interact with become a close-knit circle.

Imagine yourself a year from now. As one of my clients put it, you no longer "feel like a criminal" for neglecting the people who are most important to your business. Your clients love working with you and can't imagine life without you. Wherever you go, you hear glowing recommendations from your clients and referral partners. People are eager to work with you because they've heard wonderful things about you. And you don't have to work so hard on marketing and sales. Your services are exactly what they were before, but your reputation has grown because of your relationships.

You don't have to introduce yourself and explain what you do because people introduce you to others and follow it up with a raving endorsement. When people meet you for the first time they say, "I've heard about you." And it's always in the best way.

How do I know this works? Besides the results of my clients, I have done it. And I have *not* done it. I have felt the same pressure as any small business owner. I've been crunched for time. Cash flow has been tight. And I've put it off. I thought as long as I took care of doing these things for my clients it wouldn't matter. But I have seen the negative impact of putting it off until later. Things slow down; business dries up. And then the funds really aren't there to do these things. As they say, "Sometimes it takes money to make money." Investing funds in off-line, relationship-building marketing activities will pay for itself. When I make relationship marketing a priority, I can see the difference in my business. And I know you will, too.

Resources

This book shows service professionals and entrepreneurs how to grow their businesses by strategically building business relationships. It includes many ideas that you can apply to business. I would love to stay connected with you and support you on your journey to creating Lifelong Loyal Clients for your business, so I have some free resources for you.

Go to this link for FREE tools to help you get started turning relationships into revenues.

http://www.LifelongLoyalClients.com/BookBonus

Enjoy!

Acknowledgments

For years people have been asking, "When are you going to write a book?" And for years I didn't think the time was right. Several people contributed to making this the right time to write this book.

To Mark LeBlanc whose wise advice to write a book put me on this path.

To Kelly Pratt for providing space and structure to help me get it done.

To Dara Beevas of Wise Ink for being my "forever resource." Your wisdom, insight and graciousness transformed this book through just a few meaningful suggestions.

My editor, Henry DeVries for helping me write the *right* book.

To Louise Griffith, my Monday morning motivator and wise mentor. I saw you through your book and now you have encouraged me through mine.

And to all the amazing connections I have made along the way: colleagues who motivate me, mentors who inspire me, and clients who truly care about the people they serve and want to do it better.

Most of all to my Creator who gave me these gifts and talents and a desire to share them with the world.

About the Author

Deb Brown runs a company called Touch Your Client's Heart. Deb works with business owners who want to build better relationships and never let an important contact slip through the cracks. She speaks to groups of business owners on how to stay-in-touch and create word-of-mouth, good will in the marketplace. She has a six-year track record of working with hundreds of professionals. Her clients are more focused, able to build more trust, generate more loyalty, and stimulate more referrals.

On a personal note, she collects paper money from around the world. She and her husband are the parents of five children. She lives in Lakeville, Minnesota. To contact Deb for speaking engagements and bulk orders of this book, you can reach her at: info@TouchYourClientsHeart.com

Works Cited

"75 Customer Service Facts, Quotes & Statistics." Infographic. *Help Scout*, May 28, 2012. https://www.slideshare. net/helpscout/75-customer-service-facts-quotes-statistics/25-FACT_91_of_unhappy_customers.

Baveja, Sarabjit Singh, Sharad Rastogi, Chris Zook Zook, Randall S. Hancock, and Julian Chu. "The Value of Online Customer Loyalty and How You Can Capture It." Bain & Company.

"Bring Your CX into the Future." Walker - Customer Experience Consulting. Accessed April 19, 2018. https://www.walkerinfo.com/.

Chapman, Gary D., and Paul E. White. The 5 Languages of Appreciation in the Workplace: Empowering Organizations by Encouraging People. Northfield Pub., 2012.

Clay, Robert. "Why 8% of salespeople get 80% of the sales". MarketingWizdom.com. June 13, 2017. https:// marketingwizdom.com/archives/312

Dunbar, R. I. M. "Coevolution of Neocortical Size, Group Size and Language in Humans | Behavioral and Brain Sciences." Cambridge Core. February 01, 2010. Accessed April 20, 2018. https://www.cambridge.org/core/journals/behavioral-and-brain-sciences/article/coevolution-of-neocortical-size-group-size-and-language-in-humans/4290FF4D7362511136B9A15A96E74FEF.

Kota, Satish. "Why Customers Leave a Company." Infographic. *ReputationXL*, July 11, 2015. http://www.reputationxl.com/charts-infographics/68-of-customers-leave-you-if-you-dont-care-for-them/

McEachern, Alex. "Repeat Customers Are Profitable and We Can Prove It!" Smile.io. Accessed April 20, 2018. https://www.sweettoothrewards.com/blog/repeat-customers-profitable-stats-to-prove/.

Mitchell, Jack. *Hug Your Customers: The Proven Way to Personalize Sales and Achieve Astounding Results.* Hachette, 2015.

Reichheld, Frederick F., and Phil Schefter. "The Economics of E-Loyalty." HBS Working Knowledge. July 10, 2000. https://hbswk.hbs.edu/archive/the-economics-of-e-loyalty.

Wollan, Robert, Rachel Barton, Masataka Ishikawa, and Kevin Quiring. "Exceed Expectations with Extraordinary Experiences." Accenture.com. December 20, 2017. https://www.accenture.com/t20171220T024439Z__w__/us-en/_acnmedia/PDF-68/Accenture-Global-Anthem-POV.pdf#zoom=50

Vaynerchuk, Gary. The Thank You Economy. New York: Collins Business, 2011.

33683304R00079

Made in the USA
Columbia, SC
09 November 2018